CONTENTS

INTRODUCTION

This book is written by me, Ameenha Lee. I am a sixteen year old teenager who loves everything fashion and beauty. You might know me from my lifestyle website ameenhalee.com. I have had the inspiration to write a book for a very long time. Many high school guides for teenagers are written by adults. Many adults do not know what students in high school experience. I want to help teenagers know how to survive high school. I will help readers explore the real world of high school. I will give real advice about grades, crushes, frenemies, peer pressure, and more. If you are reading this book, I want you to feel like I am your best friend. I promise I won't make this book super boring. I hope you learn many valuable lessons from reading this book!

Before we get started,here are cool facts about me.

1.I love food.

2. Pink is my favorite color.

3. My name means trustworthy in Arabic.

4. I am currently a junior in high school.

5. I would rather skincare over makeup any day.

6. I aspire to become a Hollywood director in the future.

CHAPTER 1- CRUSHES

"The more you hide your feelings for someone, the more you fall for them"- Unknown.

If you think high school will be everything love and flowers, this chapter is not for you. Just a little heads up, the movies are nothing like high school. Do not think that you are going to be singing a solo out of nowhere like Sharpay. I know all of us girls want a Peter Kavinsky in our lives, but it probably won't happen. Boys can be real douche bags in high school. You have the guys that get super cute over the summer, but think they are Beyoncé. Next, you have the guys who love to break girls hearts. Third, you can have the super nice guys in high school. The list can go on for eternity.

Now that social media has evolved, girls stalk their crushes online. I would only recommend doing this only if you are a pro. You do not want to like a picture from 2014 on Instagram.

I will share a crush story of mine. One time I liked a guy and I followed him on social media. I decided that I was going to scroll down his Instagram to see if he liked anyone. I accidentally liked one of his pictures from 2015! I was going totally crazy. I was freaking out wondering if he would see it.

4

After my mini panic attack, I figured that I would unlike the picture. Long story short, he dated another girl that summer.

Crushes can be super hard to deal with in high school. I have had many crushes in high school, but I would rather focus on better things instead.

In the fifth grade, I liked a boy in my grade. I will just say that one of my friends told my crush that I liked him. I was super duper embarrassed at the time. That was my first major crush experience.

It is important to only tell people you trust about your crush. You can have many people find out who you like easily in high school.

For girls and boys, do not focus all your time and energy on a crush that probably won't even develop into a relationship.

Five crush tips

1. Do not stalk that particular person on social media. Many things you see on social media might not reflect someone's attitude or persona.

2. If you do not follow step one, please make sure you do not like a picture from 2014.

3. I would recommended to not focus your entire time focusing on a crush. You have better things to focus on. For example, grades, community service hours, college tours, and more.

4. If you really like a person, talk to them. It will be better to know someone's feelings than never knowing at all.

5. Do not listen to your friends. People have their own opinions about different people. One thing you might hear from your friend may be totally false!

CHAPTER 2- FAKE FRIENDS

"Fake friends show their true colors when they don't need you anymore. Be aware"- Unknown.

High school can truly change people,especially your close friends.

From my personal experience,I have had many backstabbing friends. I have had fake friends who have caused drama between my friends and I. I had a "best friend" who talked about me and thought I would not find out.

If you personally know me, I am a detective. If I would become a detective, I would solve all the murder cases. Long story short, you are going to deal with fake friends in high school. Like I stated before, people change drastically in high school. I have less friends during junior year compared to freshman year.

My personal advice about fake friends is dump them. You do not need friends who will be negative toward you all the time.

Many students in high school are becoming depressed because they feel alone. Being alone is one of the worst feelings ever. Remember that there are so many people in the world who feel the same just like you.

My personal advice is to make a lot of friends. Even if you are anti social, try to make friends. You don't want to be stuck in a situation where you lose your only friend in high school. Making friends is hard for a lot of people. You have to step out of your comfort zone and make friends. In the future, you do not get opportunities by being shy.

Fake friends= negative energy

People change change in high school due to....

1. Trying to fit in and be cool . Many teenagers try to fit in and become a greater version of themselves. Teenagers don't realize that trying to fit in changes your personality for the worst.
2. When people hang out with others, their personality can change.
3. Jealousy.. I like to call jealousy a serious disease. Jealousy can really make people do bad things. People can spread rumors about someone due to jealousy. Just a heads up, your closest friends can be jealous of you.

CHAPTER 3- GRADES

"What makes a child gifted and talented may not always be good grades in school, but a different way of looking at the world and learning"- Chuck Grassley.

Grades are super important in high school. This might not be your favorite chapter, but you will learn some valuable things. My personal advice is to take as many honors classes as you can. Me being just a freshman and sophomore, my GPA is a 3.4. You might be thinking that's super cool (yes it is and I'm proud of myself).

A weighted GPA is when your GPA is rounded up due to you taking honors classes. Do not stress yourself and take all honors classes. Since I am better at English and History, I took honors classes for those courses. Since I literally am so bad at science and math, I just took scholars classes instead of regulars. Pretty much an A+ in a honors class is much higher than an A+ in a regulars class.

Next, getting an F in high school will not ruin your life. At least take one honors class during high school to boost your GPA. Also, it looks super cool on your transcript for high school. Getting an F in all your classes is different.One F will not change your life for the worst.

On the other hand, many people have difficulty getting high grades. Many students will try their best and still not reach their highest potential. In my opinion, I always favor trying your best. Asking your teachers for extra help is super awesome. Teachers literally get paid for helping students. I love watching YouTube videos if I need any help with a hard math equation.

How to receive good grades in high school

1. Write your notes with blue ink. It is proven that blue ink helps you retain information longer.

2. Always be organized. Use folders to keep all your notes together. I would advise to use multiple notebooks for note taking.

3. Do not take classes similar to your friends. You do not want to take a honors English class if you are bad at English. Choose your own classes that fit your expertise.

4. Attempt to study ahead of time. I know that us teenagers procrastinate, but always try to study ahead of time for your exams.

5. Do extra work! You are probably looking at this tip disgusted and confused right now. Try asking your teachers for extra worksheets so you can be advanced in class.

6. Go to extra help! Teachers literally get paid to help students during school hours. Do not be scared to ask your teacher to go to extra help before or after school. I know it can be embarrassing to ask teachers questions during class.

CHAPTER 4- SET GOALS

"Set your goals high, and don't stop till you get there"-
Bo Jackson.

Setting goals is important for life in general. Setting goals in high school will help you have better motivation during high school. Setting goals for high school can vary from student to student. For example, one person might set goals to reach the honor roll during high school. Another student might set a goal to get on the varsity basketball team.

 Writing down information helps you retain it. It will also help keep track of the process you are making. Make sure to set goals that will help you strive during your precious high school years.

I promise once you start setting goals in high school, you will see a positive improvement in yourself.

Cool goals you can set for yourself during high school...

1. First, you can set goals to get better grades. If you had a C in Algebra last marketing period, try to earn a B next marketing period. Also, refer to chapter three for tips on how to get better grades.
2. You can also set a goal to join sports and clubs. Joining extracurricular activities looks super cool on your transcript for high school. I do not do sports because I literally can't even do a push up.

CHAPTER 5- BULLYING

"Blowing out someone else candle doesn't make yours shine any brighter"- Unknown.

Bullying is a serious situation that is happening every day. The statistics of students committing suicide increases every single year. If you see bullying during high school, please do not be apart of it. Your one action can change someone's life for the best or the worst. If you see bullying taking place, tell a employee at your high school. On the other hand, if you are getting bullied get help. It doesn't matter if people are telling you not to tell anyone. Life is very precious. Many bullies are responsible for students committing suicide around the globe.

Advice for Bullying

1. Stay away from all places where bullying takes place.

2. Bullying is now a federal crime. Do not think that you will get away with your actions!

3. Talk to an adult that you trust. Confiding in someone about your problems can feel very therapeutic.

4. Stand tall and be brave.

5. Do not bully back.

6. Always be confident in yourself.

CHAPTER 6- PEER PRESSURE

"I'm not in this world to live up to your expectations and you're not in this world to live up to mine"- Bruce Lee.

In my opinion, your teenage years is a very important part into shaping the person you will become. In high school you will meet good and bad people. Some of those bad people can influence you to make bad decisions during high school.

Peer pressure is known as influence from members of one's peer group. Some high schools students know how to handle peer pressure, while others do not know how to. Peer pressure can include influencing others to drink, smoke, cheat, lie, and the list goes on for eternity.

As a high school student, I see peer pressure 24/7. I remember a student in my history class had vodka in his backpack. This particular student was trying to pressure another student into drinking the vodka with him.

Many teachers will not even realize that peer pressure is happening right in their classroom. High school students already have enough stress and problems in their life already. A teenager going through peer pressure is like being stuck in quicksand.

17

Over 20%- 30% of high school students report feeling stressed due to peer pressure.

Other teenagers will choose to pressure others with a weak mindset. That is why you should always walk in the hallways with your head high everyday. Even though peer pressure is bad, you can pressure your peers to be a better person. For example, you can tell your friends to stop smoking,drinking, and acting reckless.

Your friends and peers can have a strong impact on your decisions. Many teenagers would rather listen to their friends instead of their parents. Choosing to be around the right people can change your life for the better.

Tips on how to deal with peer pressure

1. Surround yourself with positive friends and peers. Positive people are supposed to uplift and support you. Negative friends will do nothing but ruin your life.

2. If you are currently getting peer pressured, talk to a person you trust. Talking to someone you trust will help you make smarter decisions.

3. If you know someone that is currently getting peer pressured, always help a person in need. You will always need a helping hand in life.

CHAPTER 7- PROCASTINATION

"Amateurs sit and wait for inspiration, the rest of us just get up and go to work"- Stephen King.

Everyone in the world has a procrastination problem. Not cleaning your room, doing a chore, or doing a essay last minute is being lazy. Procrastination is the act of postponing or delaying something. High school students love to procrastinate so much. I know high school students that wait until the last minute to do a essay. As a high school student, I definitely have waited super last minute to do a research paper. Even though procrastination is super easy to do, procrastination is a super bad habit.

The main causes of procrastination are distractions, stress, lack of motivation, and the fear of outcome. Over 86% of students say that they have procrastinated on assignments. Also, only 25% to 50% will study for a test On the other hand, 45% of students will study for a test last minute.

Procrastination is known to cause students grades to decrease. Some students love to also watch Netflix instead of actually doing their homework.

20

Procrastination can also cause many health issues for teenagers. Cardiovascular disease and hypertension can be caused by procrastination. There is no need to worry at all! By following my steps below, you will procrastinate way less.

Tips for procrastination

1. Get organized! Organization is key during high school.

2. Create a schedule.

3. Set a deadline.

4. Take breaks. Do not take breaks that exceed two hours!

5. Set small goals for the day.

CHAPTER 8-
CONFIDENCE

"Beauty is being comfortable and confident in your own skin"

-Iman.

Adults tell teenagers to be confident all the time. Adults do not realize that being confident during this age can be hard. Teenagers have their own problems at home. Also, some teenagers can feel less confident due to social media. You might be wondering, what does this have to do with high school? Confidence has everything to do with high school.

It is very obvious when you see someone and they're not confident.

It is important to be confident during high school so you can learn how to speak for yourself. Many bullies will target people that they are jealous of. They will also target people that are not confident.

Confidence can also show through your test scores. It is better to take a test while you are confident than being scared. Confidence is a much stronger factor of success than self esteem.

Confidence tips

1.Remember that you have flaws, but you are still a great person.

2. Never compare yourself to others.

3. Love yourself unconditionally.

4. Always remember that there will ups and downs in high school.

ChAPTER 9- RUMORS

"Don't spread with your mouth, what your eyes didn't see"-
Unknown.

Rumors in high school spread like wildfire. Students in high school
love rumors. I have heard so many rumors about myself in high
school. The rumors are so crazy that I can star in my own Lifetime
movie.

Anyways, there are always good and bad rumors in high school.
Rumors in high school can make students feel like a outcast. I
have seen from my own eyes students feeling alone everyday due
to a rumor being spread about them.

People that spread rumors about other's are awful. No one should
ever have someone name in their mouth,unless it is something
positive. Rumors in high school will show you who your true
friends are. Peers that don't stick up for their friends are just fake.

Make sure to never spread rumors about people. Spreading
rumors about others will make you look super fake. This will lead
to you to becoming a untrustworthy person in your school. Also,
spreading rumors about people creates unnecessary drama in your
life. Just keep your mouth shut and you will live drama free.

Rumor tips

1. Speak up.

2. Find your TRUE friends.

3. Care for yourself before anyone else.

4. Talk to a trusted adult.

CHAPTER 10-
STAY FOCUSED

"Focus on the outcome, not the obstacle"-Unknown.

Remember that high school will be the most memorable years of your life. You need to be focused in high school in order to succeed. You can not hang out with the wrong crowd and believe you will be focused throughout high school.

Drama with other students are very common throughout high school. Excuses can also hold us back from becoming the greater versions of ourselves. Chapter ten is going to be the shortest chapter in this book. The overall point of this chapter is stay focused in high school because your future depends on it.

How to stay focused in high school

1. Hang out with the right crowd.

2. Do not surround yourself with drama.

3. NO EXCUSES.

4. Eliminate the distractions in your life.

5. Remind yourself that there will always be good and bad days.

THANK YOU..

Thank you for taking the time out of your day to read my book. I have been striving to publish my own book since I was little. I added some special affirmations at the end of this book to make your day better. I hope your high school year will be prosperous and awesome!

> I am MAGICAL
> I am GREATNESS
> I am SMART
> I am a GREAT PERSON
> NOTHING can bring me down
> I am my OWN PERSON
> I will SURVIVE high school

ACKNOWLEDGMENTS

One day I came up with an idea to write a survival guide for students in high school. This book needed serious editing for months. By the way, this entire book was edited and formatted by me! I want to seriously thank the members in my village for giving me constant support and love.

First and foremost, thank you to my beautiful mother. She always pushes me to be great. My mom has been my number one supporter since birth. Even on my bad days, my mom is always there to pick me up.

To my uncle Robert, you are one of my favorite uncles. I say that to all my uncles, but you are truly one of my favorites. Even in the hardest times in my life, you have always been there for me.

To my uncles, thank you for putting up with me no matter what. My uncles are the equivalent to my fathers. It sounds weird, but just roll with it. A huge thank you to my uncles Walter Jones, Jeffrey Sledge, CB, Hiram Smith, and Malik Gully Stoute.

To my grandma Donna, thank you for being a huge role model in my life. Even though you passed away from cancer, I still think you of every day. I love you and miss you dearly.

To grandma Bernell, thank you for being an epic grandma in my life. Also, a huge thank you for teaching me how to walk. I still cant believe that my cousins were all walking, but except me.

To Aunt Anna, thank you for being one of my favorite aunts in the world. You and Cookie are truly my favorite people in the world. One of the main reasons why I wanted to become an actress is because of you. Thank you for being a huge inspiration in my life.

To Moj Mahdara, thank you for being a mentor in my life. Thank you for supporting me throughout my journey. Also, a huge thank you to my Beautycon family.

To Richelieu Dennis, thank you for letting me be apart of the Shea Moisture family. You are a true icon to young girls around the world. Young girls embracing their natural hair is because of your hard work.

To Carly Tineo and Dinorah Pena, thank you for supporting me for the longest. You guys always go out of your way to make sure I get what I need.

To Amber and CC Sabathia, thank you for your constant love and support. Your hard work for enriching kids lives truly inspires me. I was never a huge baseball fan until I met CC.

31

Lets just say that my favorite baseball team will always be the Yankees.

To Shama and Tanya, thank you for being huge role models in my life. I look at you guys like my own aunts. I have never met two sisters who are so kind and down to earth.

To Chantal, I still cant believe you became my godmother three years ago. You are truly one of the sweetest people I know. I have also never met anyone that loves cats more than you.

A huge thank you to Vanessa. You have helped my mother and I in many ways ever since I was little. I love your whole family like they are my own.

To my uncle Pop, thank you for being my Six Flags buddy. You are one of the most funniest and daring uncles.

Finally, I want to thank my friends; my teachers; my cousins; and my god sisters.

ABOUT THE AUTHOR

Ameenha Lee is lifestyle mogul, model, journalist, and author. Ameenha Lee is the CEO of the global website with ameenhalee.com. Ameenhalee.com receives over millions of visitors monthly. Ameenha Lee has been the brand ambassador for many global brands. For example, Dr Martens, Kidpik, Isossy, Miss Jessie's and more. Ameenha Lee has also been featured in Glamour Magazine UK at only thirteen years old.

Made in the USA
Columbia, SC
02 July 2020

12964762R00021